THE BRIDGE TO ANIMAL CONSCIOUSNESS

Annie Bourke

First published in 2018 by Anne Bourke

© Anne Bourke
The moral rights of the author have been asserted.
This book is a SpiritCast Network Book

National Library of Australia Cataloguing-in-Publication data:

Author:
Bourke, Anne

Title:
The Bridge To Animal Consciousness

ISBN-13:
978-1721649679

ISBN-10:
1721649670

Subjects:
Spirituality, Metaphysics, Personal Growth, Animal Consciousness, Animal Communication, Animal Conservation

---

Editor-in-chief: **Anita Saunders**
Cover Design: **Bliss Inventive**
Photo credits: **Front cover 'Tiernay' by Zoo Studios**
Back cover (left to right) 'Reilly & Annie' by Zoo Studios,
'Paddy' by Annie, 'Naoise' by Zoo Studios

Disclaimer:
The material in this publication is of the nature of general comment only, and does not represent professional advice. It is not intended to provide specific guidance for particular circumstances and it should not be relied on as the basis for any decision to take action or not take action on any matter which it covers. Readers should obtain professional advice where appropriate, before making any such decision. To the maximum extent permitted by law, the author and publisher disclaim all responsibility and liability to any person, arising directly or indirectly from any person taking or not taking action based on the information in this publication.

Contents

DEDICATION

For Ginger, Tabitha, Smokey, Mick, Nick, Minx, Ginge, Tigger, Paddy, Reilly, Tiernay, Naoise, Lileas, Rigr, Mandla and Cecil

Thank you for helping me become who I am meant to be.

Foreword

For nearly three years I have fought for 'Justice for Cecil the Lion', not out of an obligation, but out of a need to express his final hours of torment and his fight to survive, which continued for 40 hours after he was wounded. His spirit has always driven me, and the connection I feel to him is strong. This was intensified when the world lost the last male northern white rhino, Sudan, in Kenya in March of 2018.

It has been difficult to count the permanent losses of endangered species during the past five years. To know that this has become "acceptable" is concerning. To know that this is happening in my lifetime tears at my soul. Sudan left a permanent mark, as did Cecil, but how much more will we lose before humanity wakes up?

The message the animals send is one of hope, of strength, and reassurance that we can and should continue to speak for them, for generations of wildlife to come, and to protect not only their legacy, but to define the way we as a world treat and honour them. When we lose that, we as a people have nothing.

I am grateful for Annie's words, which reinforce within me my resolve to continue the fight. When we open our minds, we open both our hearts and our souls.

Thank you Annie for being an inspiration.

Maureen Dauphinee

Founder – Justice for Cecil the Lion

Introduction

In the Beginning

Animals were created for a reason. In the Bible's Job 12:7 we are told "but now ask the beasts, and let them teach you, and the birds of the heavens, and let them tell you". We are here to serve as stewards for the land and custodians of the animals. Animals are living beings with souls who experience emotions just as humans do, and should be shown respect, consideration, and compassion. Understanding why they are here, and what guidance and knowledge they have to offer us through communicating with them will enrich our lives and theirs, and ensure that their legacy lives on.

Animals are my passion. I am committed to being an advocate for them, and being their voice.

With the chronicling of the creation of Earth, God[1] (Source, the higher power) brought the animals into being before humans. Humans were created to co-exist with the animals, to look after them and share the

---

[1] I will use the word 'God' throughout this book, but please replace this with whomever or whatever term is meaningful for you.

planet with them. Throughout the Bible there are numerous references to animals: the animals at Jesus's birth, the Lamb of God, the lost sheep, Jonah and the whale, lions, donkeys, camels, dogs, the pairs of animals on the ark, snakes, crawling creatures, owls, oxen, eagles, horses, wolves, cows, ravens, and sparrows. It is no coincidence that they are mentioned so frequently; we need to recognise and understand their significance and importance.

Animals have permeated many aspects of human lives. In the archaeological sites of Göbekli Tepe in Turkey (reputedly one of the oldest human sites found to date) and the Pyramids of Giza, there are numerous depictions of animals in stone engravings, in addition to the enigmatic sphinx. There are animals featured in national coats of arms and crests, they appear in children's stories (e.g. Pooh, Eeyore, Tigger, Lassie, *Cat in the Hat*), in musicals (e.g. *Cats, The Lion King*), and movies (e.g. *Red Dog, Puss in Boots, Madagascar, Zookeeper, Life of Pi, We Bought a Zoo, A Dog's Purpose*).

We have animal prints used for clothing, bedding, shoes, handbags, and accessories. We have toy animals and animal jewellery. We have animal symbols for cars (e.g. Jaguar, Holden, and Peugeot). In Australia we have a polar bear as the symbol for a locally made rum. We associate storks with babies. We use some animal types as derogatory terms (e.g. pig, cow, mongrel, bitch, dinosaur) which these animals consider as disrespectful, rude, and thoughtless. We have integrated the animals' stereotyped characteristics into our daily language phrases (e.g. "dog tired", "cheeky monkey", "memory of an elephant", "raining cats and dogs", "snail mail", "free as a bird", and "having a whale of a time").

Although we may not be consciously aware of the reasons why animals are such an important part of our lives, at a subconscious level we are affected by them in many ways.

It is my life's purpose to share my experiences and knowledge and assist you to expand your heart, mind, and soul to a greater level to appreciate the wisdom, guidance, humour, and love you can experience from being with and communicating with animals. This book is not a how-to guide for animal communication; rather, it highlights the benefits of animal communication as a means for better understanding animals.

There is a huge gap in human knowledge and understanding about animal consciousness. It is the intent of this book to raise awareness about animals, to help you have a richer relationship with domestic animals, to improve appreciation of animals in ethical captivity, to highlight the plight of our wild animals whose numbers are diminishing at an unprecedented rate, and to advocate for animal wellbeing across the planet.

It is my hope that this book will make a difference for animals at a domestic household, national, and international level. I trust that this book creates the cross-species bridge so that humankind can better understand animal consciousness, and have a united vision and commitment to give them greater care so that they exist for generations to come.

CHAPTER 1

Soul Journeys

Why are animals on the planet? We, as spiritual beings, have chosen in this lifetime to have a physical experience on Earth as humans. Like us, animals have souls, and they have similarly made a soul contract to evolve through experiencing a physical life on Earth. They have chosen to incarnate in animal form. They may have had human lives prior to this. Some humans have memories of past lives as animals. Some animals come back as the same animal form in different life experiences; two of my cats have had previous lives with me as cats, and one has had a human relationship with me in the past.

Just for clarity, my understanding of past, present, and future lives is that they are not linear, which is a thought-provoking concept for our rational, logical, scientific brains to comprehend. From my personal experience and experiences with my cats, soul aspects can experience multiple lifetimes simultaneously, in different dimensions and different universes, or parallel universes. My girl cat Reilly passed away unexpectedly, but explained she had done this so that she could return in a new kitten body as a higher frequency and more highly evolved soul version of herself. This allows her to continue teaching and guiding me through experiencing this phenomenon with her. She orchestrated a powerful example of the soul aspect reality so I would know and share this insight. I continue to communicate with her Reilly aspect, and with her new kitten identity. They are different aspects, but the same soul existing at the same time in the physical realm and in the spiritual realm.

Animal souls may be here for the same reasons as our souls are: to deal with karma (energetic debt) from past lives, to learn specific lessons (e.g. survival, overcoming hardships, learning to be independent, appreciating family, developing relationships, parenting, not taking things for granted, having to trust and rely on others, coping with a disability), and ultimately to experience love and to progress on the soul ascension path through opening their hearts and the hearts of those around them. Anyone who has had a pet experiences unconditional love which is the greatest gift they can give. They trust us to look after them, they develop strong bonds with us, and return the love and affection we show them in many ways, even if we are not consciously aware of this. We can't demand affection; they bestow it on their terms. For some humans, experiencing unconditional love from an animal may be their first conscious experience of this special heart-activating frequency. Even if they only share a short part of our life journey, we are the richer for them choosing to spend their life with us. There is no judgement or criticism from them; what we look like first thing in the morning, our moods, our sadness and tears, our choice of clothes and our friends. They can see who we really are under the facades and masks, they accept who we are, and they love us forever.

Some animals come into our lives to help share our burdens, even though we haven't asked them to do this. It is a great and selfless act of love for animals to take on physical illness symptoms and diseases for their humans, so that we don't have to experience the full impact and consequences ourselves. With their intuition, they know what is happening in our systems, and can start exhibiting signs of their human's disease even before the human is showing symptoms at a physical level. They see it as providing a service for us and that it is their responsibility to do what they can for us, even if they sacrifice their life in the process. My cat Reilly kept getting throat chakra symptoms which she was taking on physically for me as I wasn't progressing fast enough on my soul path. I needed to be speaking my truth and sharing my gift of animal understanding. When I worked out what was going on, I asked her to stop taking on these health issues for me. I told her that I wanted her to be happy, healthy, and whole, and that by being ill on my behalf was adding to my stress levels. Being so committed to helping me, she asked "Are you sure?" to clarify that I really did want her to stop being of service to me in this way.

Just before finishing this book I developed severe fevers and a respiratory infection, and disturbed the cats with my violent coughing. After a few days, my cat Tiernay was not himself and wouldn't disclose what was wrong, so I took him to the vet. He had an extremely high temperature, and a respiratory infection. None of the other cats were ill, and he hadn't been anywhere to pick up an infection. When I queried if he had taken symptoms on for me so that I could recover more quickly in preparation for getting the book completed, he said "it was a pleasure". I thanked him for doing that, and asked him to get better as soon as possible so I didn't have to worry about him. Thankfully his temperature came down very quickly and he has returned to good health.

It was noble of him to help me but stressful waiting to find out what was actually wrong and then waiting for his symptoms to improve. He wasn't keen on spending two days with the vet and hid on the second morning in the hope I wouldn't find him and he wouldn't have to go. His hide-and-seek game was eventually foiled, and he had to go and continue his treatment. I don't think he'd quite thought out the implications for him of taking on my health issues. Many animals are not keen on visiting the vet, like some humans not being keen on going to the dentist. I have successfully used a couple of essential oils to calm them, particularly for long car trips.

Some of our animals are here to protect us: they can sense the presence of other energies and guard us from harm. They keep the vibrational frequency of our homes at high levels. Often they sense and see things we cannot, and perhaps it is better that way! They will be particularly attentive and close to you if they feel that you are at risk.

Many animals have come to teach us. For some people, it may be that having the responsibility for caring for a pet is the only way they learn to look beyond self-absorption and focus on another being to improve their lives, and they will grow from experiencing unconditional love during this process.

Whales and dolphins are understood to be carrying ancient wisdom which can be accessed by those who need to work with that unique knowledge as part of their life purpose. There were whales and dolphins playing in the bay near the island guest house where I finished this book. It was such a thrill watching the dolphins playing in the waves, and sensing and appreciating their energy of fun, frivolity, and freedom. The whales told me that "sharing wisdom is an honourable achievement" which was sage advice for those of us there writing our books.

Your pets may be here to teach you specific information you need to fulfil your life purpose. When I first asked my cat Reilly to start teaching me, she said "About time!".

Reilly has vast knowledge about crystals and healing: she knows which crystals people and animals need for their individual circumstances, and is accurate with everything when I have checked with a variety of sources. The first crystal she told me about was rhyolite, which I didn't think I had heard about before. I looked it up in my crystal guide book, and it wasn't there. Since I was a novice animal communicator I doubted that I had heard correctly what she had said, assumed that the crystal did not exist, and did not seek further clarification. Many weeks later I was checking an old handbag searching for something, and pulled out a string of crystals which I had bought a long time ago. When I looked at them, the tag said rhyolite! I didn't remember seeing the tag when I bought them; I was just drawn to them. With an apology to my cat I searched for rhyolite online, and found all of the information easily. It is also known as rainforest jasper, and had been in my crystal book all along. When I read the metaphysical properties, I understood why Reilly had started my crystal education with this particular one. It is the "communication stone" for cats! As teachers the animals are patient, but also know what we need to know, and have a time frame for keeping us to task! Their mission as teachers is to help us succeed with our life mission.

CHAPTER 2

Being an animal's human

Whether you are caring for animals at home, in a refuge, or a zoo, you will work out fairly quickly that they are not "your" animal: you are "their" human! You don't own them. As their human carer, they expect you to provide for them – food, water, toys, entertainment, clean litter trays if they are indoors, and visits to the vet (often reluctantly on their part till they appreciate it is for your peace of mind and their good). Grooming can be a battle of wills; they may think they are quite capable of looking after themselves, thank you very much.

Most of all, animals want your love, care, companionship, attention, and time. When they love us so much, they are bemused when we spend most of the day at work and come home tired and stressed and tell them about our day. The obvious question is, why don't we just stay at home with them? Everyone would be much happier. Having one-to-one time with you is their ultimate pleasure: having your undivided attention, not competing with the television or your mobile phone, but having your complete focus – it is all about them. We provide love, and we interact verbally even though we may be blissfully unaware that they understand everything we are saying because we can't understand their vocalisations (until we master animal communication).

We are expected to be interactive entertainment units, with moving toes and fingers regarded as potential prey, and playing footsie through the bed linen a favourite pastime. My youngest cat channels a polar bear and lands on my feet with a colossal impact of several kilograms of airborne furball, then tries unsuccessfully to bite my toes through the doona. We are interesting targets for climbing practice, bearing scratches and scars from unsuccessful mountaineering attempts. A young female cat was obsessed with biting me. I've never had a cat wanting to bite so much, which took me by surprise. It took some time and lots of conversations to convince her that she did not need to bite me and that she could show her ownership of me in more human and socially acceptable ways. She then resorted to sneaking up behind me when I was seated, wrapping her front legs around my neck, and gnawing my hair! Animals love to groom us to show that we are part of their tribe, sharing their scent with us, and exulting if they score a lick on your nose!

You will eventually be resigned to the fact that anything that is yours is theirs, and anything is a potential toy. If you have something that is particularly valuable, you need to hide it away effectively. They can open doors and drawers, and stare at the fridge as though they are willing it to open. My boy cat Paddy used to love "rescuing" my knee-high stockings and socks from the laundry basket and moving them all over the house. When younger, Tiernay constantly stole my watch no matter where I hid it and would carry it around like prey and play hide and seek with me, and would put bracelets and necklaces out of jewellery boxes into my bed – a genuine cat burglar! Fortunately he appears to have grown out of that habit. My youngest cat is obsessed with hair bands and has hidden them around the house, and I am still trying to work out where they all are!

Ping pong balls are great for cat soccer, and cardboard boxes of any size are great for beds and cubby houses. Cats in particular like to feel secure so will squash into tiny spaces and feel snug, or jump up high where they feel safe. I have a range of cat beds and boxes around the house, and invariably someone will be curled up in the smallest available offering, including the largest cat who does a contortionist act to sleep in the baby cat bed. For indoor cats, buying cat grass has helped with their digestion and it disappears in a flash after an orgy of chomping. Climbing frames and palaces are a wonderful investment for kittens and cats to entertain themselves, and a test for humans to assemble them with minimal instructions while watched by furry supervisors eager to play. Jumping, hiding, playing with dangling toys, and defending your real estate from rivals keeps everyone occupied.

Getting exercise is also important for animal development and wellbeing. As well as running around the house, animals relish being "outside". You can train cats to walk in dog harnesses (just don't tell them it is a dog harness) from about four months. There are kitten harnesses to start them with and then you can progress to the sturdier dog harnesses. Paddy loved going for a walk and would run to the front door to get his harness put on when I verbally asked if he'd like to go for a walk. Since he was a lot bigger than a lot of the dogs we met while walking, it was interesting to see the reactions of the dogs and their humans. We even had a car that passed us reverse back just to check that they really had seen a large cat going for a walk on a lead! I have lived near terribly bored dogs in several places: they bark incessantly and must drive their owners crazy, but they are just trying to tell their humans that they want to go for a walk, see the scenery, and have some play time. Spending all day banished in the garden on workdays, even with toys, is not as stimulating or fulfilling as spending time with you.

I am compelled to share some animal safety advice with you. It really surprises me that a lot of people are not aware of everyday risks for their animal friends. As a responsible carer for an animal, you are obliged to keep their environment as safe as possible for them and limit what they can accidentally knock over when you aren't there to supervise. You also need to know what plants and food are not safe. All members of the lily family are toxic for cats, and since cats can jump just about anywhere, it's safer not to have them in the house and not have them growing in the garden if your cat goes outdoors. Please be careful if you receive flowers that there are no lilies if you have a cat. Please advise your florist not to include lilies of any kind if you are buying flowers for a household with cats. I recently received some flowers and I was suspicious that there were some small lilies in the mix. When I rang the florist, fortunately they had a record of what had been sent. The florist looked up the information about the suspect flowers, and discovered that they were dangerous for cats, so I had to remove the lilies from the house.

You also need to be aware of the toxicity of human foods for animals. Many people like giving animals scraps, but some of our human foods can be fatal for animals. Please consult your vet for comprehensive food safety advice for the animal you care for. Common advice includes no chocolate for dogs, and no onion (raw, cooked or powdered), garlic, grapes or raisins for cats or dogs. Please stow plastic bags, empty food bags that smell delicious, and bags with handles safely away from animal sight and access to prevent misadventure.

Paddy loved perfumed roses: he would assist me in the garden while I was weeding and pruning, sitting draped over my shoulders or lying on my back and supervising. I had one place on my kitchen bench where I could wedge a vase so it couldn't get knocked over by the cats, so I would fill it with roses and fill the house with scent. Invariably I would come home from work and there would be a solitary rose in the middle of the kitchen floor. Paddy would look at me with very innocent eyes as though saying "It jumped out of the vase all by itself" or "It's for you". I called him my "sensitive new age cat" and he spent years perfecting floral rearranging with roses and carnations.

Although animals do respond to scent, another safety issue is the use of essential oils with animals. I only use therapeutic grade, 100% plant-based essential oils for humans and animals. There are a lot of essential oils on the market that are not therapeutic grade, and may have synthetic components or alcohol in them, which reduces their therapeutic value. Please do not burn essential oils in a burner: this can be toxic for both animals and humans. There are a number of oils that your animals will not tolerate and there are safety precautions for different species, so please check with your vet or animal aromatherapist before using essential oils. Therapeutic grade oils can be safely used to support animal health with the appropriate oils and methods of use specific to individual health needs of the species.

Your animals will also "help" you with your chores. If you want to write something, they will be fascinated with your pen and try and steal it as a toy, or sprawl all over your documents and go to sleep so you can't access what you need to. If you are working on a computer, they will drape themselves over the keyboard and add some extra letters for you in your typing. If you have been sorting stuff out and have piles of papers or clothes to move, someone is likely to come along and pounce on them and move everything to the floor for easier sorting! I had bought my father a double-sided jigsaw puzzle of cats to be the ultimate tease. He had patiently sorted all the pieces into different coloured cats, when our cat Mick hopped onto the jigsaw and disturbed all the piles. Mick also liked helping my mother to sew. He was intrigued with the scissors moving through the fabric and loved to watch, although from a safe distance.

Animals love to be alarm clocks and jump on you mid-dream when it's time for you to get up and serve them breakfast. Fortunately my cats are accommodating and tolerate occasional late dinners and let me sleep in on weekends if I ask them to. Many are creatures of habit and like their meals at set times and will definitely let you know if you are late. Paddy expected breakfast and dinner promptly at 6.00. They also love to help cleaning – mine are intrigued by a floor duster / mop device and hop on for a ride, which makes the task more difficult pushing around several kilos of wonderfulness on the end of the mop! Paddy stole the limelight at a cleaning product party and would not leave the mop alone. The sales consultant had not experienced anything like that before.

Animals have different personalities, just like humans. Some will want to be the alpha males and females, and may not want to share their kingdom with other animal members of the same sex. Some of them may not want to share you with other animals or humans. Others are happy to keep the peace and stay out of the way of younger or more active animals. My gorgeous girl Reilly was a dominant female, and everything was done on her terms. She was very independent, which was atypical for her breed, and showed affection when she wanted to. I kept telling her that I loved her and that I wanted to show my affection for her, and gradually she became more gracious about allowing me to cuddle her and stroke her. She loved being above me, either lounging on the back of "her" recliner chair with me or lying on top of me, so that she was still on top and therefore the dominant female. It is so interesting seeing the world from an animal's perspective.

You need to be aware that any changes in your behaviour will affect animal behaviour. If you suddenly spend less time with them or show less affection, they won't understand that you have an extra-busy time at work or have just met a new potential partner and are pre-occupied. They will think that they have done something wrong and have upset you. They may try to misbehave because they will know they will get some response from you for doing something naughty, and sometimes any interaction and attention is better than none. Some will respond by following you diligently and silently demanding that you notice them and give them some attention and love. Some may become withdrawn and lose their appetite because they think you don't love them anymore and will pine. When they are used to your habits and behaviour and you change them, you definitely affect their world and they can't make any sense of it. Even if you are extraordinarily busy, you still need to make time for them and time for showing affection so that they are reassured and know that their relationship with you is strong. They rely on you for emotional support just as they emotionally support you. It's a two-way relationship and all parties need to respect that.

Some animals will have extra-special needs, and will require extra-special carers to nurture them and help them. Animals who have been abused or abandoned carry deep emotional wounds just like humans, and need someone with patience, tolerance, and willingness to help them build trust again. I have spoken with animals who have been abused, or who have been separated from their human family not of their will, or who know their humans can no longer be their carers. These circumstances are deeply traumatic and animals can carry these emotional scars for years. Some have shared graphic images of their abuse and it is heartbreaking to know they have had such appalling experiences. It is then just wonderful to see their life change with an injection of love and frivolity and kindness as they heal in new homes with humans dedicated to helping them overcome their past and making them feel secure, wanted, and loved. Animals with disabilities or injuries also need special humans to care for them and support their rehabilitation.

Some zoos are now focussing on providing animal enrichment, with plants, scents, hidden treats, and toys in their enclosures to provide stimulation and elicit normal behaviours. This is similar to what we do with domestic animals but on a much larger scale. It's fascinating to watch orangutans playing hide and seek with bits of cardboard and fabric, lemurs swinging on ropes, and tiger cubs playing in pools and chasing moving toys and their keepers!

Despite their idiosyncrasies and occasional patience-testing behaviours, the labour of love experienced when caring for an animal is absolutely worth it. It is a big commitment to be a carer of an animal, and you invest much love, time, and money to provide them with a quality life. The rewards are invaluable: you get their loyalty and trust, there is scientific evidence that animals are good for your health (reducing blood pressure and stress), they don't criticise or judge your choice in clothes / hairstyle / partner / accessories / tidiness, they listen solemnly to all you want to share, and the greatest gift they offer is unconditional love; unwavering, unbounding, and endless. Being a carer of an animal is a gift to accept with open arms and an open heart. Humans have a great capacity to love and feel emotions, and so do animals. For those of us fortunate enough to have animals sharing several lifetimes with us, I believe that the love bond is even more evident. I understand that the love relationship with an animal is eternal, both during lifetimes and between lives. Love endures.

CHAPTER 3

Communicating with animals

For years I had communicated verbally with my cats as if they were human, and sensed that they understood what I was saying, but I wanted to know what they were saying to me. I used to tell them that I knew they knew and understood what I was saying, and wished that I could speak "cat". I had experienced a number of animals making vocal sounds (calls, chuffs, purring, growls) and expressing themselves through their body posture, ear positions, and tail positions; much like humans absorb the verbal and non-verbal cues and messages from other humans.

For me, with animals it is their eyes that draw me in; an intimate connection between souls, a recognition of souls, and a unique, respectful bond. This is very rewarding even if just for a few moments with a dog walking by, pets waiting at a veterinary clinic, or animals in a zoo.

In our daily lives we seem to forget to really connect with the people around us. We tend to avoid sustained eye contact for more than a few seconds or offer a reassuring pat, but with our pets we tend to mimic their sounds, and spend a lot of time verbally interacting, playing with them, hugging them, and sharing moments of affection. The old adage that "the eyes are the windows to the soul" is just as relevant with animals as with humans: while staring into their eyes you can feel a powerful link and know that through this bond they are trying to tell you something. Some seem to will you to take action or will you to be aware of their need to communicate through gazing at you intently. Some show their appreciation or affection by a lean against your body, a brush with their tail, a mild head butt, a lick, a deliberate wink, a gentle pat with a paw — their version of an animal hug and a thank you for loving them, looking after them, and sharing a relationship with them. They know instinctively if something is wrong, and will spend time very close to you to provide comfort. Sometimes they do really whacky things to make you laugh and smile, and ease tension. They definitely can sense your mood barometer.

Although we can communicate with animals on a physical level through vocal verbal communication and touch, there is another level of communication where we can more effectively express ourselves and, more importantly, understand what they want to tell us. This is communicating on a telepathic level: mind to mind. Apparently we do this automatically when we are young children, but grow out of it. If you watch young children with animals, they do have conversations, and the children can tell you about the animal. The good news is that as adults we can reactivate this communication channel and experience very enriching conversations and deepen the bonds and relationships with animals, whether domestic, captive, or wild. There are animal communicators all over the world offering courses to assist animals and their human carers to communicate, which will change the dynamics of your relationship immeasurably.

My family welcomed a litter of kittens when my old faithful companion female cat Tabitha disappeared in her 19th year. Our new adventurous boy Nick and his two sisters provided hours of entertainment and were affectionate and good company while I was awake late at night studying and doing assignments, falling asleep beside me on piles of textbooks and photocopied articles. Sadly, one by one, they departed their earthly lives to reunite on the other side. The last girl who passed away, Ginge, had been my special girl, the runt of the litter and a ginger female, which was unusual as most ginger cats are male. When she passed away, held in my arms, I was determined to find out more about animal communication. Some time later, searching on the internet, I found a website in Australia advertising an animal communication course. Uncannily the image on the website was a double for my Ginge! I felt that this was no coincidence. Everything happens for a reason and I felt my gorgeous girl was guiding me to this site and confirming that this was what I was supposed to do. After reading the coursework outline, I enrolled, and a whole new world opened up for me.

I now had two cats who I felt were very human with their vocal communication and their very expressive eyes. Night after night Paddy and Reilly assisted me with the course work. I was busily practising sending them messages and images and being open to receiving responses and images back from them. Animals are extremely sensitive and intuitive, and know exactly what is going on around them, and they say it exactly how it is, no holds barred! They show images like little movie snippets to answer questions, or answer directly. Be warned: Paddy used to spend my shower time sitting on the closed toilet seat waiting for me to emerge to continue with his hug therapy. Embarrassingly when I took him to an animal communicator / energy healer for a session, he shared the images of the shower scenes when asked what happened during his day!

Their individual personalities are a delight to behold, as are their senses of humour. One of my girl cats used to delight in telling me that she had produced a hairball while I was at work. After falling for it the first time and looking everywhere for the non-existent mess when I got home, I would question if she really had done one. "Wait and see" was the response in an amused tone. Their voices are individual like human voices, and they speak in different tones as necessary.

I often chat to a friend's dog who was a rescue dog and quite traumatised before moving to her new home. It has been illuminating talking to her and reassuring her that she is safe. She is so calm and confident now that she shows me herself physically laughing. She loves lying on her back when she is at a dog-friendly café to get attention and tummy rubs and distract her humans, and head butts their groins like a charging bull as a way of saying "I love you, you are mine".

As an animal communicator, you need to respect the animal you are trying to talk to, and ask permission to talk to them. It is their free will if they choose to talk to you, and sometimes they don't want to. If this is the case, accept it, and send them positive wishes. Perhaps next time you ask they will be ready. I introduce myself and say that I am practising animal communication and ask if they would be willing to talk to me. If they don't respond the first time, I ask again in case they need to accommodate to the human telepathic communication (which is different from their telepathic communication within their species), and if they again don't respond, I thank them and move away.

I have visited lots of zoos and chatted to lots of different kinds of animals, and there haven't been many who didn't want to talk. Most have been surprised, then appreciative of having someone who can talk to them, wanting to spend time with them, asking how they are and finding out if anything needs to be done to make them feel better or more comfortable. I can then pass messages on to keepers and all the ones I have chatted to have been quite open to animal communication and have accepted the messages gratefully.

As I am a keen animal photographer, after talking to an animal I often ask them if they would mind turning to face me so I can capture the eye-to-eye soul connection of the interaction. It is amazing and rewarding when the heads turn to look directly at you — they know exactly what is going on. I chatted to a koala who had his head turned side-on to me the whole time during our conversation, but at the end when I invited him to turn to face me, he swivelled his head around, gave an exaggerated wink, and let me take a lovely portrait to remember the moment.

If you ask animals questions, you need to be prepared to be told the truth, even if you find it unpalatable. When visiting a zoo as part of an animal communication workshop, we, as participants, had to ask a crocodile about her favourite food. Unexpectedly she answered "humans". I said "You can't say that" and she replied "You asked the question, I'm giving you the answer!" Although she was born in captivity and had always lived in zoos, she had obviously communicated with her colleagues in the wild and understood that humans are the most delicious meal available.

I had an unexpected experience trying to talk to a talking cockatoo at a zoo. He talked aloud saying "Hello" but I tried talking to him telepathically, which is silent. He ignored my two requests to talk, so I moved around and explored the rest of the zoo. When I walked by his enclosure again, his keeper was in there chatting to him verbally and tidying. When the keeper left, I said "Hello" out loud. He responded, saying "Hello, hello". So I said verbally "So you want to talk out loud do you, what would you like to tell me?" He looked at me carefully, raised his wings and his comb, and then screeched and screeched and screeched as though something absolutely awful was happening, then folded down his wings and comb, looked directly at me and said "Ha ha"! True story! Just like humans, some of them are real jokers and pranksters.

We also need to be mindful that animals understand everything being said around them, to them, and about them. There are recognised cases where animals are unhappy or exhibit unusual behaviours because they don't like their derogatory or negative names humans have bestowed on them. All words have a vibrational energy and when spoken aloud as a sound form, if this is not positive and the animal hears it all the time, it affects their energy field, and ultimately affects them. As humans, we may get upset, angry, or resentful if someone says something rude or dismissive or unflattering about us, and the same goes for animals. The crocodile I spoke to about her food preferences revealed telling advice:

"We think we are beautiful, and we have feelings too." We can only guess what comments about their appearance they have overheard and been insulted by.

Being conscious of the words you use and the tone you use makes a difference in the relationship with your animal. Even if they act aloof or independent and ignore your requests for affection, they understand perfectly well what is being said, and will show affection on their terms, in their time, when they are ready. Telling them that you love them (even when they push your buttons doing the things you've specifically asked them not to do, like jumping on the television stand) has a very profound effect on them, and you will see their behaviour change as they respond to what you say. Sometimes their soul lesson is to experience love, and they have come into our lives for us to help them achieve this.

How much more empowering it is to ask animals what they would like to be named! My younger cats have chosen their names and my cats who have reincarnated have chosen their new names too. For me it is fascinating that they comprehend that the phonetic spelling of the name is different to the pronunciation, so have deliberately told me what the word looks like when spelt, rather than what it sounds like, so I can find the right name. It has been a special little mystery mind puzzle to solve each time.

Animals like playing games with you too – puzzles to make you work out the answer rather than doing all the work for you. I guess it is their way of making you learn and remember important things. My cats often tell me words to answer my questions but sometimes only the starting letters and I have to decipher what they are telling me, and then they give confirmation. They are very knowledgeable about healing with crystals, and give me clues about crystals that either I need to work with, that they need for their health, or that people or animals I know need to work with. When I check for details in my crystal book, I am amazed by the accuracy of their recommendations.

Once you are on the right wavelength to talk to animals, you can chat from anywhere in the world. Whenever I travel now, I tell my cats in advance that I will be going away, where I am going, when I am coming home, and that I will talk to them every day. It's very reassuring for everyone to know that all parties are okay, and prevents unnecessary anxiety.

Telepathic communication is also invaluable for finding out what your animal likes and doesn't like in their everyday life, and if there is anything wrong that they are happy to share. In my experience, cats hide pain, and don't like to worry their humans about health issues. Sometimes they don't want to tell their human what is happening, so you may need to consult with another communicator to discover what is really going on. You can find out their food preferences and what they do and don't want in their food bowls, their favourite toys, any other needs, and their favourite activities with you. Once you can communicate effectively, then they can start teaching.

My first Maine Coon Paddy showed me via telepathic video snippets that two of his favourite times were when I arrived home from work and walked through the internal garage door, and when I sat on the recliner chair for our cuddle and Reiki sessions. The first words he told me were "sore left hip": clear as a bell. There had been no sign of any problem with his hips as he would jump onto my lap and onto furniture. When he had his X-ray, there were significant arthritic changes with both hips, with the left much worse than the right. With regular Reiki, other vibrational therapies, and anti-inflammatories, he continued to be an inspiration and radiated love.

One of the first dogs in the spirit world I communicated with during mediumship training showed me a lovely multi-coloured material ball, with different materials pieced together like segments of an orange, being batted around furniture legs. His human confirmed that this was his favourite toy. He also kept telling me "chocolate, chocolate". When you receive messages from animals, whether visual or in words, it is tempting to rationalise or try to explain or interpret or doubt what you've seen or been told. It is very important that you pass the message on as received and the receiver will understand it. I thought that chocolate was an incorrect message as dogs are not supposed to eat chocolate, but as he was so insistent on passing this message on, I told the owner that he was going on and on about chocolate. She laughed and admitted that at the time she didn't know it wasn't healthy for him, and it had been a special treat for the two of them to share a bar of chocolate.

Animals are very perceptive when your behaviour changes, and must be particularly sensitive to changes in our emotional bodies, sensing a change in the vibration in our energetic field or aura, as they can detect when something is wrong. I was asked to talk to a dog whose behaviour had completely altered from vibrant and happy to morose. He had been prescribed antidepressants, but was not making progress. When I spoke to him, he said there was nothing wrong with him, but his human was the one with the issues. She had lost three close friends in a short space of time, and was grieving, and not doing her usual pattern of activity, including her usual interaction with him. Once his human received assistance managing her depression and grief issues and renewed her normal verbal chatting and play time with the dog, the dog's behaviour changed within 24 hours. He was safely weaned off his medication and both are back to their usual selves.

I am not advocating that animals should be medication free, but would like vets and animals' humans to be aware that there may be emotional factors affecting animal behaviour, and these need to be addressed to bring about a change. It may be that the animal is stressed or unhappy, is affected by changes in their environment, is affected by their human's medical symptoms or emotional state, or that something else significant has changed in the animal-human interaction. Through investigating what these factors are by communicating with your animal, you can improve their health and happiness, which also benefits yours!

CHAPTER 4

Saying hello

Choosing a new animal companion can be a challenge when you already have pets. Some can be very territorial and may not want to share their space with an 'intruder'. Some are very protective of you so may feel that you are at risk with a stranger in the house, and may become very clingy and not want to share you. Some may feel that they have done something wrong and that you don't love them as much and need someone new to love, and their behaviour and demeanour may change quite drastically as they perceive incorrectly that your love for them has diminished. Accepting a new animal into the family is a big deal for animals, so imagine their reactions to bringing new human companions home! It is really important to tell animals that you don't love them any less, that they have done nothing to upset you or change how much you love them, but you have capacity in your heart to love a new family member.

In my experience it has been invaluable to consult with the existing animal family before deciding on a new addition. Having gained their approval for having a new animal, you can then discuss their preferences for the animal's sex, name, when they are arriving, safe sleeping space / territory for them etc., which allows acceptance and adjustment prior to the arrival and also enhances the integration process. It has also been helpful and stress reducing for all involved to talk to the new family member before they arrive so that they know about the home they are coming to, know something about their new human, and develop the relationships with you and their new siblings in advance before they arrive. All of this benefits the introduction and settling-in phases.

Although I had two beautiful and loving Maine Coons approaching 11 and 10 years, I had felt for some time that there needed to be a third cat for completion of the family on a spiritual / metaphysical level as well as on the physical level. I knew I needed a red-coloured cat. I didn't know why, but that's what I instinctively knew I needed. I discussed this with my two resident cats. My male cat Paddy didn't mind if the new family member was male or female, and he had no concerns about having another cat join the family. My female cat Reilly, on the other hand, was adamant it had to be a boy – she was the dominant female, the alpha female, and was not going to tolerate sharing her throne with another female!

Having gained their approval for a male, I found a gorgeous red kitten online. We then discussed names, and had a selection to suggest to the new kitten, who then chose his own name and the less common spelling of the name – Tiernay. As well as my frequent conversations with him before he was ready to leave the breeder and his mother, Tiernay also had conversations with Paddy and Reilly, and had established bonds with all of us before he walked into the house. He was very excited about coming to a family where the human was able to speak "cat".

With only a few hisses from Reilly to welcome him, Tiernay settled into his new home and family in a couple of days, sharing a cat bed with big brother Paddy, chasing Reilly all over the house, and then the reverse (she was a really good sport playing with him and it looked hilarious having a four-month old kitten chasing a ten-year-old cat), and amusing everyone with his energetic antics and busyness with his toys. It was interesting to watch their occasional family meetings – I didn't listen, but could see them all silently communicating and letting him know what was what.

When Reilly passed away unexpectedly (detailed in the "Saying goodbye" chapter), the boys knew what was going on. She had told them what she was doing. They didn't appear to pine, and acted as usual. When I asked how they were feeling, they said that they were fine, and that it was just a temporary reprieve before she was back to boss them around again! They knew she was coming back, and we just had to wait till she came back. When she was ready to join us again as Naoise (pronounced Nee-sha, and yes, she picked her name), within two days she was eating food out of the boys' food bowls, draping herself over Paddy to get groomed as she had done in her Reilly incarnation, doing her unique individual behaviours and sitting on her favourite chair back where only Reilly had sat. All was peaceful and it was as though she had never left us.

I appreciate that these introductions have been seemingly easy, and I attribute much of that to being able to communicate and prepare everyone beforehand. Not all introductions are like this. I spoke to an elderly cat whose family were keen to get a dog. They had not consulted with her and when I broached the subject, she replied "over my dead body". I knew there was going to be trouble in paradise, and warned the owners that she was not receptive to having a dog in the family. Their other cat had passed away and she was enjoying being in a one-pet household. Sadly, her health deteriorated and she passed away. The family was then able to welcome their new dog without upsetting anyone.

Another older cat I chatted to did not like having a new kitten in the house, even though she knew her humans really loved it, and still loved her. There was no private territory she could have as her own – the kitten was everywhere. It is important to try and have a safe area for the new animal to feel secure, and somehow manage to have areas where the established animals can have some peace and solitude. Sometimes you can talk and explain as much as you like, but they will only tolerate each other to a point, just like humans! They all have their own personalities, and just as we don't turn every acquaintance into a best friend, neither do animals. We have to respect them, and trust that a truce can be negotiated.

Choosing a name for your animal is just as important as choosing names for your children. There are meanings to names and particular energy vibrations with the names which animals are aware of. Giving animals names with a negative connotation can affect their psyche and behaviour, as the global YouTube phenomenon of the black jaguar called Diablo (devil) demonstrated. Diablo had been mistreated at his previous location, and was justifiably concerned about what was going to happen at his new home. When he discussed with an animal communicator how his name affected him, along with his traumatic background, he was reassured that there were no expectations about what he had to do in his new home, and his name was changed to Spirit. The video footage shows that Spirit's behaviour, attitude, and interactions changed markedly following the sessions with the animal communicator, and changed the views of many sceptics about the authenticity and benefits of animal communication.

Some people may doubt that animals understand name meanings or know their names or understand everything that is going on around them, but from my experiences they are very wise souls. They know the names humans have bestowed on them, they can communicate with their own species around the world, and can provide expert commentary on contemporary issues affecting animal and habitat conservation. I spoke to a cat called Mitey, and the first thing she told me was that she did not have an infestation. She disliked her name with the connotation of mites, and had a selection of "olde worlde" names prepared that she would prefer for her name. I spoke with a tiger cub who thought her name was too formal and too "old" for her, and wanted to be called a diminutive which she thought was much more attractive and endearing.

You can ask an animal what it would like to be named, or give it some choices. I have a Celtic theme going with my cats honouring my Irish ancestry, and have researched endless lists of Irish and Celtic baby names and historical names and the meanings. Tiernay was offered a selection of names starting with T to consider, and fortunately liked what he chose. When Reilly passed away, I asked her if she wanted to be called Reilly again when she came back – she wanted her new name to start with N and told me it would read like Nais / Ny-ese when I found the correct name. After weeks of research I found "Naoise" which is pronounced as "Nee-sha" and is quite different from how it is spelt. She knew if she had told me the pronunciation I wouldn't have found the correct name.

To help settle the new cats in their new home, I've asked what crystals they want, and have had these in the car for their journey home, and then in their sleeping area. I have also used essential oils to calm them and welcome them, like the biblical anointing of years gone by. As I advised in Chapter 2, you do need to know what you are doing when using essential oils with animals and ensure you use 100% plant-based therapeutic grade oils. Not all oils are appropriate for animals, and there are certain ways to use oils to safely support animal health. I have completed a course in animal aromatherapy and am a certified clinical aromatherapist (for humans) and am very careful with oil blends and dilutions to prevent harm and support health for both animals and humans.

When the new animal arrives home, it's less stressful if they can have a space of their own and get used to their surroundings and the new smells, before being confronted with their new animal family. The established animals will be inquisitive about the new arrival, and may watch their movements with keen interest. Your new family member will need to be shown the basics such as where the food and water are, and where their litter boxes are. It helps considerably if they have been toilet trained before they arrive. As well as acclimatising and familiarising themselves to their new surroundings, your new animal also has to get used to foreign noises. Hearing a hair dryer for the first time, your mobile phone ring tone and alarm, the doorbell, the vacuum cleaner, a flushing toilet, and various kitchen appliances can be frightening until they understand it is part of your daily routine, and they gradually accommodate to the sounds.

Welcoming new humans into the household can be equally distressing or stressful for animals, who have to adjust to the new energy in the house, unfamiliar smells and noises, and a change in your behaviour and daily activities. Some animals cope well with a human baby and can be very protective. Others can be scared or upset with the unpredictable crying, and resent the amount of time you are spending with the baby instead of them, and may exhibit unusual behaviours to make their feelings known, e.g. using the baby's bedroom as their bathroom! When there has just been a small family unit and the animal has had your undivided attention for some time, it is a huge adjustment to share you with someone else. Again, it is important to reassure the animal that you still love them, that you will have to change your routine, but you will still make time to be with them. Animals also have to adjust to babies learning to crawl and walk – dealing with them when they are in a cot and not mobile is quite different to having them scooting around the house and chasing them. They will be intrigued with baby toys and will think they are for them. I bought a baby frame with dangling toys for my kittens and they loved swatting the toys and spinning the wheels on the support struts.

Bringing a new adult human home also changes the household dynamics. If the animal family has been used to having you all to themselves, it is a big change when another human comes and stays, whether family, friend, or partner. It takes time to adjust to having someone new in the house, which can be a challenge if you have a timid animal or one recovering from previous abuse. They will need to get used to the scent of the new person, their voice, and their movements. Spending time with the animals to reassure them that everything is okay and that your love for them has not changed is important. They may not like who you bring home, but you are the one they have the unconditional love relationship with, and maintaining that relationship is essential for their physical and emotional wellbeing.

CHAPTER 5

Saying goodbye

The loss of an animal at any age can be just as emotional and devastating as losing a human loved one. Our animals are regarded as part of the family, and a huge part of our lives, whether we are aware of it or not. Even if they are "naughty" fighting with each other, chewing things they shouldn't, shredding mesh doors, or surprising us with the occasional nip, we love them. They might be a working animal, a companion for someone on their own, or a cherished and adored pet. Unconsciously there is a powerful bond on both sides. They comfort us during hard times, they amuse us with their antics, they show us great affection and unconditional love, never judge us, and relish playing with and being with us. We can take great comfort with a cuddle or hug with them – they know instinctively when to snuggle near you, jump on your lap, and soothe you.

Dealing with losing them is not easy. Sometimes it is unexpected, like a car accident or a heart attack, or something progressive like battling a terminal condition. Whatever the cause, we have to cope with the loss of them in the physical world, and adjust to not seeing them in their usual places, not hearing their vocalisations, and not feeling their warmth and vibrations of breathing or purring or barking.

Grief is something we all deal with individually and differently, and it takes time to heal the hole they leave in our hearts and the indelible impression they leave on our souls. We mourn, we reminisce with photographs and videos, and despite the pain, we can be grateful for their presence in our lives and the joy they have given.

From the experiences I have had talking with my own animals who have passed over, and other animals I have communicated with, their passing over process is similar to that of humans. They transition to their spiritual being, undergo healing, and energetically can stay very close to their humans. I have heard numerous times of experiences people have had with their animals in spirit who have manifested strongly enough that their humans can hear them and feel them and sense their presence. I too have experienced this, and find it very reassuring that our animals can be witnesses to life after death, or life after life. Although we can't see them in the physical realm, we can be comforted to know they are often nearby and with us in spiritual form.

Although they understand that we are sad when they leave and that we need to grieve, they find it hard to see us so unhappy. They accept it is an acknowledgement of how much we value them, but are concerned with unintentionally contributing to their human's emotional turmoil. They don't like seeing us distraught and heartbroken, and they aren't able to be with us to comfort us physically. Like humans, they have a destiny, and sometimes their timeline is shorter than we would like. Sometimes we don't get the chance to say goodbye and thank them for the immense happiness they have brought into our lives. Words are not necessary – they understand the emotional bond. They don't want us living with guilt or regrets for not saying how much we loved them, or thank you, or apologising for raising our voices when they misbehaved. They understand everything that we say, and the unsaid things: they are intimately aware of us and our issues on so many levels. No animal I have spoken with who has passed over has held any grudges for their humans not getting the opportunity to say goodbye.

Helping an animal to pass over is also a difficult time. Some animals are not strong enough to pass over on their own, and need assistance. Some would prefer to pass in a familiar environment, but appreciate that it may not be possible. I spoke to a very unwell cat who knew her time was imminent. Although she wanted to stay at home, she accepted that she had to be taken to the vet and was incredibly grateful for her owner showing this great act of love in helping her to go and ending her suffering. She reassured me and her owner that she would be close to him in spirit form, and that he would feel her around his legs.

As previously mentioned, I had the experience of cuddling Ginge, one of my cats, as she went to sleep – savouring connecting with her eyes and feeling her in my arms for one last time and knowing that her lovely soul was free to reunite with her brother and sister who had passed over years earlier. She has appeared in numerous meditations since to guide me and let me appreciate and be reassured that she continues to thrive, as do my other animals who have passed over.

Experiencing an animal dying unexpectedly is a huge shock. You just take it for granted that they are going to be part of your life for years, and suddenly they leave with no time to say goodbye. I got up one morning and my gifted girl Reilly (who taught me so much about the healing properties of crystals) was in her bed having a very serious conversation with her brother. I was feeling weird after being knocked by a car on a pedestrian crossing a few days earlier – fortunately I was physically unscathed but was shaken on an energetic level. I noticed Reilly looked a bit grey and asked her if she was okay and gave her a pat. She seemed okay so I went to the kitchen to get the cats' breakfasts organised and she started screaming with a tone I'd never heard before. I thought she had a claw caught in her bed and released it but she continued to scream. I rushed to get ready to take her to the vet, not knowing what was wrong but knowing she was extremely distressed, but she passed over quickly while I was doing this, and was lifeless when I picked her up a few moments later. I was already recovering from the surreal experience of being hit by the car, and now know that she intentionally picked this time with care so I would better manage dealing with her unexpected departure while I was in the process of my energetic recovery, and also because she knew she had the perfect opportunity to come back.

Since she had been communicating with me for so long, I just assumed that she would keep talking when she got to the other side, but had no idea how long she would take to go through the transition and healing phases before she had enough energy to come through. I had so much to ask her, including why she had passed so suddenly. I also had to find out if she wanted to be buried or cremated. I'd never had to ask before – she was the first cat who'd died since I'd learned to communicate with animals. Since she was such a special cat I was relieved when she spoke not long after she passed. She said she needed a new body – very matter-of-fact, as though that was a perfectly normal thing to do. She also said she wanted to be cremated, and that she wanted a brass urn with a particular shade of blue that was significant for her, with silver. She also kept saying "MI MI" and I thought she was trying to tell me about a crystal as she knows so much about crystals and their healing properties. I didn't understand at first, and then I worked it out – myocardial infarct. She'd had a heart attack, which the vet confirmed. She had no history of cardiac illness and hadn't been ill, so it was a huge shock when she passed so quickly with no warning.

I spoke to the staff member at the animal crematorium about an urn with the details that Reilly had requested, but they only had a blue pottery urn with gold trim. The lady very obligingly told me she had seen something similar to what Reilly had requested on eBay. I had never bought anything from eBay and wasn't going to start with purchasing a funeral urn, but put in "animal funeral urn" as a search term online and found a business in Australia (Furry Souls) specialising in urns for animals. On their second page of urns was a brass urn which was hand painted with the correct blue hue enamel and inlaid with nickel flowers in a pattern called "forget-me-not". It was exactly what she wanted and she knew I would find it. She also told me which crystals she wanted in the urn. I bought them and when I checked in my crystal book, they are used for heart attacks, providing more confirmation that it really was her talking to me!

Reilly also told me to stop being so sentimental! She knew she was coming back as a kitten, and told me the pattern and fur colours, and the cat breeder where I would find her. Her brothers did not appear worried she had disappeared and weren't looking for her or off their food or moping – they understood it was a temporary hiatus till she was ready to join us again. She had obviously told them what was happening and she visited us a lot in spirit form. I could sense when she was in the house and the boys certainly knew. I had no idea how long she was going to take before coming back in physical form and she didn't give any hints. She had told me two days before she passed that her time was soon, but didn't indicate quite how soon that was! It certainly made her death much easier to cope with knowing she was coming back, and was a test of faith and trust waiting for her to come back. Since she had been so accurate with other things she had told me, I had to believe she was telling me the truth, even though it seemed so incredible. I'm sure a lot of my friends and colleagues thought I was crazy waiting for her to return, although they were too polite to say so.

I contacted the breeder who I had purchased one of my boys from and said that although it was going to sound weird, she was going to have a kitten born with certain colourings and it was very important that she came to me. The breeder was quite accepting of this and said she would inform me when the kitten arrived. I sensed she was conceived on a full moon which was lovely synchronicity as I was born on a full moon and love the energy. I was about to go overseas and was anxious not to miss her, and the breeder reassured me that she would let me know when she had my kitten. On the day I arrived back in Australia the breeder emailed me a photo of a kitten who had been born consistent with the date when I felt that she was conceived. She had the right colours and pattern, and it was definitely her!

I met her at six weeks and am blessed that she chose to come back and keep working with me and spending time with her brothers. Since the boys recognised her on a soul level, she settled back into the family very quickly, and although now the youngest in the family, was still the dominant female! I know not everyone is as fortunate to have their animals come back in the same human lifetime, and I am sure she has done this so I can write about it and share the joy and reality of eternal existence. I know a number of animals have had previous lifetimes with their owners and it is such a gift that they choose to come back and spend more time with us in physical form. I know Reilly could have stayed in her spiritual form and continued to teach me, but what a wonderful experience to have her come back again and be able to hold her again.

When they do come back, their souls are at a higher evolved level, so they aren't exactly the same. They are operating at a higher vibrational frequency, and my cats who have come back are obviously running at a higher temperature now as they radiate heat. They may look extremely similar or completely different, but you will recognise something that is very familiar – the eyes, the way they move, where they sit, how they look at you, and idiosyncratic behaviours that only they did the last time that they were here. There is something on a soul level that you will recognise and resonate with. Ignore the opinions of others who regard you as deluded or irrational. You have an incredible bond with your animal and you will know without a doubt that they are back. My cats have proven for me the eternity of the soul, and that reincarnation of the soul happens. They have let me experience these events so that I can share them and help others cope with their grieving processes through knowing that life goes on and that they can communicate with their animal on the other side. In addition to adjusting to and accepting these miraculous events, it has been fascinating watching the whole family dynamics change over time, as the older family members come back as the youngest ones, and everyone's roles change. Tiernay was the youngest and the energiser, and now he's the responsible big brother.

I know I am in a very fortunate position to be able to communicate with my cats and other animals in the physical and the spiritual realms. It is lovely to assist bereaved humans by connecting with their animals in spirit and passing on messages of love and confirmation of the soul's ongoing existence. It is so beautiful and emotional to hear the animals talking about their humans and passing on messages of gratitude to support the healing process. Although some humans may feel it is disrespectful to bring a new animal into the home soon after an animal's death, animals I've conversed with understand the grief process and understand that having a new family member to love is a powerful way to move forwards, and doesn't detract from the love they experienced or dishonour their lifetime and pride of place in family history.

Whether you have an animal in your life for a short time or a long time, they hold a special place in your heart, and although it is inevitable that one day we will need to say goodbye, it would be wonderful if they could stay physically for our whole lifetime. Like our human family and friends, we never know when their day of passing will come, so we have to learn not to take them for granted and treasure the time we have together. Go for walks, play, don't yell when they sleep on the good lounge, hug them often, and tell them you love them. They understand what you are saying and will show their affection in myriad ways: a wink, a gentle lean against you, a soft swishing of their tail against you, resting their head on your lap and gazing at you, vocalisations, kneading you, or jumping on you for a cuddle.

When you have known an animal for a considerable time, sometimes you can identify subtle changes in their behaviour when they aren't well, although some animals are stoics and can hide serious illnesses till the last minute because they don't want you worrying unnecessarily.

Paddy was my first Maine Coon cat – an absolutely adorable, loving cat who relished going to sleep in my lap. He was very tolerant with my forays into animal communication and being the recipient of Reiki, crystal therapy, and essential oils as I developed my knowledge of modalities to support animal wellbeing. He was all about unconditional love – teaching me, his siblings, and all who met him. He was really wise and shared some of his past life experiences with me as part of my spiritual development. He had had human lives, including as a priest in ancient Egypt, had had a life as a cat with me in ancient Egypt, and was a gifted healer and seer. He knew much about energetic healing, crystals, and essential oils, and taught me so much to equip me for my life purpose. He is one of the most human-like cats I have ever met.

I had thought quite early in our relationship that I wouldn't be able to bear having him euthanized when the time came – I loved him so much and wanted him to be able to pass over naturally when it was his time, rather than me having to end his life. I had always told him I wanted him to stay as long as he could, and he reassured me that he wasn't going to be "kicking the bucket" for years to come. He passed the average life span in good health, but after a few more years started to decline, and I took on doing some of his routine care which he was no longer able to do. Since he had given me so much love and care, I told him I was happy to look after him as long as he wanted to stay. I didn't want him to stay and suffer for my sake, and wanted him to tell me when he was ready to leave. I didn't want him struggling or in pain, but wanted him to stay as long as he wanted to – his choice, on his terms. We continued to have lots of long cuddle sessions and I adored holding him in my arms next to my heart, gazing into his all-knowing, all-seeing eyes. He continued to vocalise and communicate telepathically with me.

Unexpectedly one morning he didn't eat all of his breakfast which was unusual as he had had a good appetite and always emptied his food bowl each meal and drank his water. Nothing else was out of character and he didn't say that anything was wrong. When I got home very late that night, he didn't want any food or water, and made strange vocalisations I'd never heard before. He accepted water from a syringe in his mouth – I didn't want him dehydrating.

My heart was breaking: after years of having him as my mentor, friend, companion, and family, he was telling me it was his time to go. I had to prepare myself to say goodbye. I didn't know if he would last the night or drift off in his sleep. I got his favourite crystals and we had a long cuddle session and I had the chance to thank him for being in my life for so long, for guiding, supporting, and loving me, sharing his wisdom, and for staying as long as he had. I laid him gently in his bed. The next morning he still refused food and water, and gave a few more cries to let me know that he really needed to depart his earthly life.

Our vet was on holidays, but one of our lovely veterinary nurses who knew Paddy very well was on duty, and she looked after us with care and compassion. All his body systems were closing down and in failure. Helping him to pass over was the kindest thing to do. It was a lesson for me to understand that even though it was something I hadn't wanted to face, it is a great act of love when you let someone go, to free them from potential suffering and respect their wish to pass. He went to sleep peacefully with me patting him. He was ready to go and be reunited with his sister, and he knows I will love him for eternity. It's normal to feel grief, regret, or guilt when they pass – did you do enough, should you have picked up that something was wrong earlier, should you have told them more often how much you loved and appreciated them? He didn't want me worrying about him and hid everything about his health issues till the last possible moment. Yes, I went through a huge grieving and healing process, and have released even more grief writing about this experience, but if we didn't love our animals so much, their death would not affect us so much.

The animals I've spoken with who have passed over understand the sorrow and trauma we experience as they transition to the other side. With Reilly passing it was a huge shock – she was alive one minute and gone the next. I didn't realise she was dying and didn't have a chance to say "Thank you for all you have done for me and taught me"; "I love you so much"; and "Goodbye". With Paddy I had a night and a morning;

time for final photos and a cuddle and saying what I wanted to say. My advice to help in advance for saying goodbye is to take as many photos and videos as you can throughout their life. Your grief may be too raw to face looking at them immediately after their death, but when you are ready, they will evoke such happiness and joy having your loved one perpetually alive. I just recently found a video of Paddy taken years ago which I'd totally forgotten filming and it was just beautiful listening to him vocalising and feeling that he is still here.

It doesn't get any easier saying goodbye to an animal. Each time the grief seems overwhelming and you are surrounded by reminders of them – their bed, toys, food bowls, and photos, but not that living, breathing, loving being who means so much to you. The loss of their physical presence is hard to adapt to, and life can feel very empty, but our animals don't want us being distraught with grief and mourning. When animals pass over, like humans they transition and go through a healing phase, reunite with other human and animal family members, and often come back and stay very close to us in the spiritual plane. A number of people have felt, heard, or seen their animals in spirit when they visit, and your other animals will definitely be aware of their presence. If they are staring intently at something that you can't see and they are not bothered, it's likely that your loved one is there.

Many of my cats who have passed over have visited me in dreams and meditations. I can hear them vocalise, see them as healthy and healed, pick them up and feel I'm actually holding them, all of which has helped with the process of dealing with their deaths. As an animal communicator and animal medium, I have been able to continue talking to them after they have passed over, which has significantly assisted me with the grieving process. Although I can't physically see them, I know they are there and they are willing to continue guiding and teaching me. I have also been incredibly blessed to have the souls of two of my cats come back in different bodies as kittens again in my lifetime.

To my knowledge, not all of our animals reincarnate in our lifetime, but I've spoken with lots of people who have recognised their animal back in a new body. It is such an act of love for them to want to come back and continue a physical relationship with us, and continue to teach, guide, protect, or whatever their life purpose is the next time around. For those of you who have seen the movie *A Dog's Purpose*, this depicts exactly what has happened with my cats: they pass over, they come back. The soul endures, and love endures.

These animals could just stay on the other side and communicate with us, so it is a powerful gesture of love when they choose to come back again in physical form to be with us. As higher evolved forms of their souls, they may look different and behave differently in some ways (as they will have integrated their soul lessons from their last lifetime) but you will know with absolute certainty who they are. Both my cats who have come back told me what they would look like and picked their new names, and have surprised me so much with their very similar appearances and uncanny mannerisms that it has been a challenge not to call them by their original names!

If it is not their destiny to reincarnate again in our lifetime we are currently experiencing, we have to be grateful for the time, experience, and lessons learnt with them, and look forward to the possibility of being reunited in another lifetime. Paddy showed me that we had shared a lifetime in Egypt thousands of years ago when he was an Abyssinian cat working in the Great Pyramid. We may not understand how our souls travel through the dimensions of time and space, but I appreciate all the cats in this lifetime who have chosen to be with me, am grateful for the wisdom they have shared, and look forward to what they reveal in future lifetimes.

It is a privilege to share our lives with these wonderful beings, and despite feeling the pain of the world ending when they leave us, we can move forward knowing that they are safe and contactable on the other side. They appreciate our care and love, and know that reunions are possible. When we pass over, we reunite with them. For the here and now, knowing that there is life after life and that the soul lives on is a powerful tool for recovering and healing so that eventually we can get our hearts ready to invite another animal into our lives and build an enduring, loving relationship all over again.

Paddy had told me before he passed that he would come back. I didn't know when. After the experience with Reilly, I knew I would have to be patient and wait. My mantra now is "Anything is possible. Miracles happen. Dreams come true". My miracle happened and my dream came true: he has come back!

CHAPTER 6

Animals in zoos, protected parks, and reserves

There is contention about whether we should be keeping animals in captivity and protected reserves or if we should leave them undisturbed and truly free in the wild.

Zoos, parks, and reserves don't have the land to fully replicate the normal habitat sizes that animals would roam through in the wild to find food, find a mate, and raise families.

Despite this, there are a number of advantages for animals living in what I call "ethical, conscious zoos", where animals are respected and valued, and their health and wellbeing on all levels is imperative. In these types of zoos, animals are:

- Protected from predators, human harm, and habitat loss

- Provided with nutritionally appropriate food, with periodic "starve" days for certain species to replicate their normal feeding patterns

- Able to access uncontaminated fresh water year round

- Monitored with veterinary care on hand

- Participants in carefully planned breeding programs, which when successful maintain gene pools and reduce the risk of species loss and extinction

- Sheltered from weather phenomena

Efforts are being made to enrich their environments and provide stimulating activities to maintain normal behaviours and quality of life. Hiding food, repositioning toys, and spraying other animal scents keeps the environment dynamic and helps elicit normal behaviours and action.

Having animals being more accessible to people in zoos, parks, and reserves allows for greater connection, understanding, and appreciation of animals. Most people would never have the opportunity to go on safari and experience animal encounters in the wild. Zoos provide education about animal species and their plight in the wild, they raise awareness of at-risk and vulnerable species, and can generate support for ongoing conservation and welfare efforts through fundraising, donations, and links to partner conservation organisations.

As an animal communicator, I love going to zoos and having conversations with the animals and taking photographs. They are happy to share information about their life and may disclose information about issues so that these can be passed on to their keepers to rectify. It is lovely when there aren't too many other people in the vicinity. It feels as though it is just you and them in a private world where there is a focussed communion of souls and exchange of thoughts.

One of the most powerful connections I have experienced was with a grizzly bear in the Seattle Zoo, years before I started formal animal communication. I love all animals but have a particular affinity for big and small cats, and all types of bears. When I went to the bear enclosure, there were no other humans around. The bear had a large enclosure with grassy areas, and a pool with a glass wall so you could see him in the water. I watched him for a while and took lots of photos, then moved to the viewing glass next to the pool. He must have known I was there because he came and stood up against the glass facing me – we were facing each other separated only by an inch of glass. It was the most phenomenal, profound experience being so close to a wild animal and having the spontaneity of the connection. He came over to me for a virtual bear hug.

I spoke with an emu in an animal park. He was in an enclosure with lots of trees and the ground was extremely muddy after heavy rain. This wasn't replicating the normal emu habitat. I asked him if he would like to talk to me and he said verbally "Whoomph, whoomph". He was speaking "emu" to me. I told him that I was very sorry but I didn't understand emu, and asked if he could please talk to me in English, or show me pictures to convey his message. He changed to English and told me how unhappy he was in the enclosure, as he wanted to run around in grassy plains. The situation has since changed. The park has closed, all of the animals have been relocated, and the emu is now content.

Something that really challenged my thinking was talking to animals in nocturnal houses. These are animals who are active in low light, so are housed in a dark building with very low lighting so that people can see the animals moving in their enclosure. The animals said that they were "crepuscular" which was a term I'd never heard before, and means that they are active in low light at sunrise and sunset, and are used to the fluctuations in lighting to guide the biorhythms of their body systems. In the nocturnal house, it is dark throughout the day, and then it is dark at night when the humans go home. The animals get minimal variation in the amount of light, and do not get to experience a normal day's worth of light variation from dawn to dusk, which disturbs their circadian rhythms. Living in the constant dark is not ideal and not good for their wellbeing. I believe zoo staff need to rethink how they house these animals so that they can experience some periods of light and facilitate normal body cycles.

I spoke with a little furry Australian native animal called a dunnart. He was in a glass enclosure in a nocturnal house next to a snake. Although there was frosted glass on the lower section of their shared wall, on an energetic level the dunnart knew for certain that the snake was next door and was living in constant fear that the snake would come through the wall and consume him. It was not doing his health any good living in a state of constant stress. Again, I think zoo staff need to consider the emotional wellbeing of animals and not inadvertently cause them unnecessary tension and strain with where they locate them.

When I visited Taronga Zoo in Sydney for the first time, it had been pouring with rain early in the morning, and the rain was just starting to ease and the sun was coming out as I caught the ferry across Sydney Harbour to the zoo. With the horrendous weather at the start of the day, there weren't the usual number of sightseers at the zoo, so I essentially had the animals to myself as I walked around. There was an absolutely magnificent snow leopard in an enclosure. He had cliffs to climb and a cave to hide in and space to move around. He had beautiful eyes and stared at me intently during our conversation. He was happy being there, but said he was lonely. I sent him lots of love and moved on to talk to other animals. When I came back to visit him in the afternoon, he moved right down to the front of the enclosure to be closer to me. It was just wonderful having that connection and having him recognise me and choosing to be nearer. All of a sudden one of the doors in the side wall of the enclosure opened, and in ran a second snow leopard! The energy changed completely as they chased each other all over the enclosure with amazing aerial acrobatics, leaping and pouncing. I was so happy for the snow leopard that he had a friend to play with. It was such a joy watching them playing carefree and really enjoying themselves.

I had booked an encounter to meet two young tiger cubs with my dad, with the money going to tiger conservation. I didn't feel that the animals were being exploited, and it was a great opportunity to raise awareness of dwindling tiger numbers in the wild, and meaningfully contributing to efforts to preserve them. I'd introduced myself to the cubs and had been chatting with them prior to visiting them, so that they knew we were coming. They shared lots of details about their daily life, and told me that their favourite toy was a ball. On the day of the encounter they were full of beans, cheeky and wanting to explore and play. We were allowed to stroke them on their backs, but when I was near them they would roll onto their backs as though inviting a tummy rub, which we weren't allowed to do. The keepers kept coming over to roll them on their tummies again, and as soon as they left, the cubs would roll on their backs again. It was lovely witnessing their antics. Disappointingly there was no ball in the encounter area. I wondered if I'd misheard them, and doubted the accuracy of what I'd been told.

Some time later the cubs were put into another play area so that they were on public display. Their keepers were in with them and playing with bits of rope and other toys. All of a sudden the ball made its entrance – it was a basketball, or perhaps I should say it had been a basketball! It was nearly flat and well chewed and obviously well loved. The cubs would bite an edge of it and the keepers would pull it and them – they literally had an absolute ball playing with the ball. It was so entertaining watching them playing – the exuberance of youth and seemingly unlimited energy and curiosity.

At Chester Zoo in the United Kingdom, I was keen to see the lions. There were a huge number of school children on class outings, and several were at the lion enclosure. It was a hot day and the lions were resting so we couldn't see them properly. The children were roaring at them and yelling at them to get up, but the lions ignored them and kept relaxing. Once the children had moved away, I connected with the male lion and asked if he would mind sitting up so that we could see his face. He obligingly sat up and looked straight at me, and I took some very special photos of him. A lady standing next to me said "He's looking straight at you" and I said that I had asked him if he would. It's a free-will situation – he didn't have to sit up, but he chose to. I was very grateful for the experience and the wonderful memories the photos now evoke.

I personally get energised by being around animals, and am very happy seeing them well looked after and enjoying life. You don't need to be an animal communicator to have these connections. To me it is rewarding making that unique connection with an animal: a treasured moment in time. My advice is to relish the experience of meeting these wonderful beings.

CHAPTER 7

The Lions' share

I have had the opportunity to connect with white lions, lionesses, and cubs in several places around the world. They are very rare, and are very special souls.

In South Africa I met a most majestic white lion, who was happy to share his wisdom, and was one of the most wise and serene souls I have ever met. I sent him lots of love, and he told me he was returning it threefold. Being the recipient of that intensity and warmth of love was almost overwhelming: such a powerful force of pure love. He gave me so much guidance while sitting near me; a melding of minds to transfer knowledge.

He has since passed over; however he continues to guard and guide. I spoke with him after he passed over, and the following is his explanation about white lion wisdom and the purpose of white lions that he wanted to share with you:

"The white lions carry the frequency of divine love and purity. They are amplifiers, guardians, way show-ers, protective and prophetic. They imbue the highest vibration of love for transformation and transmutation of lower energies. They are here to support the new evolution of humans in their higher dimensional frequency. Tawny lions ground and stabilise Earth energies, whereas white lions work to transcend pain, suffering, and darkness. White lions are emissaries of peace and ambassadors of love. They are white light in physical form."

"They carry etheric codes for Earth's re-energised blueprint. They guard gateways to the galaxies and other dimensions. They raise the frequency of the light quotient – the love energy frequency needs to be raised for true peace and everlasting unity."

"They call to the spiritually conscious, and to those still awakening to their spiritual being and purpose. They roar approval to encourage our efforts. The essence of soul evolution is love. Love lights our auras up so we can shine like beacons for others."

When I asked him recently if there was anything else he wanted me to include in this book, he said:

"There is hope. I am grateful that there are so many dedicated humans committed to changing attitudes and investing in species survival. Thank you for not ignoring the warning signs. This is the critical time to take action. Time is not on our side. We need an investment in science, research, agriculture, tourism, and local regulations to solve animal conservation from multiple angles. Please continue this essential work, and don't give up. The animal kingdom is relying on you."

How profound, and how fortunate we are to have such wonderful, selfless beings walking the earth with us, willing to communicate what we don't know and need to understand.

The death of Cecil the lion when he was lured out of the safety of his reserve caused an international uproar. In the aftermath, the outrage led to a tsunami of action to review laws about importing animal body parts, with some airlines and some countries banning them. The impact of trophy hunting was exposed; however one of Cecil's sons was also hunted and killed not long afterwards.

Losing the lead male means a significant change for the lion pride. A new male takes over, and usually he kills any remaining cubs so that only the cubs that he sires live and continue his gene pool. The females have to deal with the loss of their protector, mourn the loss of their young, and adapt to having a new dominant male. The killing of one lion may have a cascade effect, resulting in multiple deaths within the pride, and causes huge emotional ramifications for the survivors.

Cecil was very noble and humble when I spoke with him shortly after his death.

He said:

"We each have lessons to learn in our incarnations. I endured suffering so that many would not have to. My passing has seen a chain reaction of action and advocacy for animals. More needs to be done about illegal trade of animals, body parts, medicines, and poaching. Much has been achieved with habitat preservation, eco-tourism, livestock protection, alternative community income from protecting animals and land, advocacy, species conservation, media, and research."

When I invited him to add any further comments for this book, he said:

"Money alone won't solve the problem for us. We need intent, drive, passion, commitment to working together, altruism, global collaboration, and enduring will to achieve meaningful change. For wild animals to have a future thriving in the wild, we need humans to unite and support our rights to live and thrive. We want our future generations to exist in safety and witness freedom. Blessings."

My wish is that more of us speak up for animals as they really rely on us to speak on their behalf. We need to be a voice for the voiceless. We need to listen to what they want to tell us. May we continue to make a change for Cecil so that his death was not in vain, and may we honour and emulate his selfless gifts of forgiveness and love. May Cecil the martyr's legacy live on through his grandchildren and through the spiritual guidance he continues to share. May the global impact his death caused continue to drive efforts to better protect and achieve conservation of animals in the wild.

CHAPTER 8

Overcoming extinction

Animals are becoming extinct and are on the edge of extinction due to mankind's actions, and inaction.

One of the biggest threats to animals that humans are responsible for is global warming. Our age of technology and our inability to effectively control greenhouse emissions are affecting our environment: land, water, and air. This has significant impacts on animal habitats. This can be seen dramatically in our polar regions. It is so distressing to see the effect on polar bears, who are having to change their behaviour and lifestyle to swim long distances searching for food, which exhausts them and wastes their valuable energy reserves. They are starving to death due to the impact of weather changes on sea ice formation. Our ice caps and glaciers are melting and retreating at alarming rates. In Antarctica icebergs are melting and have the potential to markedly raise sea levels.

Our arid areas are also changing, with more droughts, changing rainfall patterns and rising temperatures. These events result in diminished water reserves yet animals have to have access to water to survive. There are unsung heroes in Africa driving water trucks to the animals to keep them alive.

There has also been a major impact on the marine ecosystem. The rising global temperatures are causing rises in sea levels and sea temperatures, which are damaging the marine ecosystem and threatening viability of marine life. In Australia the coral reef systems are suffering due to global warming. This is resulting in coral bleaching and altering the biodiversity of the reefs.

Another concerning man-made environmental risk for animals is pollution. Our waterways are polluted, and marine animals are dying from ingesting our plastic waste. We are responsible for cleaning up our mess. Fortunately there are organisations committed to cleaning up our oceans, and innovative approaches to recycling waste are being implemented world-wide.

Our relentless search for natural resources and extraction methods such as oil drilling are putting pristine wilderness areas and their resident animal populations at risk, with the media spotlight currently on Alaska and the Congo. The demand for palm oil continues to grow, despite the degradation of habitats with deforestation and the encroachment of roadways. In Indonesia this is having a significant impact on orangutans, Sumatran tigers and rhinos, pygmy elephants, monkeys and sun bears who are all on the path to becoming critically endangered. As well as trying to cope with the impact on their habitats, the animals are easier targets for poachers and live animal traffickers as the jungle areas are now more accessible. There are also implications for animal health and survival with the burning of undergrowth and unwanted timber.

From cosmetics to food to biofuel, palm oil has become increasingly used in our daily life, at a significant cost for animals. There is valuable scientific work being done to develop biofuel substitutes which have less impact on the environment. Efforts are also being made to look at using land more efficiently and farming more productively to create more yield with less land, which can only help animal survival. There is significant marketing underway promoting saying 'no' to palm oil products. There is a big industry associated with producing palm oil, and producing this palm oil is causing big problems for animals.

We are facing a global crisis with threatened, vulnerable, and endangered species; species and subspecies facing extinction; and species that we have lost due to extinction in the past few years. We have areas in Africa where lions, elephants, giraffes, rhinoceroses, and cheetahs are now extinct, and the lions and tigers than once roamed Asia have all but disappeared. Some species and subspecies now only exist in zoos.

A part of me did not want to have to write this chapter as it is so emotive, sobering, and, for me, soul-destroying to contemplate what humankind is doing to the animal kingdom. It is the dark and disturbing side of life for animals, but it is a reality that has to be exposed so that something positive can be done about it. It is not my role to pass judgement on those who harm, traffic, or kill animals for sport or profit or questionable research; however, I can speak on behalf of the animals affected by these practices and share their experiences through their poignant words.

I acknowledge that these issues are contentious and that there are massive industries and livelihoods associated with these activities. We have graphic images bombarding us relentlessly about the plight of animals being poached and trophy hunted, the inhumane killing of hundreds of whales for "scientific research", the atrocious conditions that live export animals endure, the mistreatment and exploitation of animals, the impact of the shoot-to-kill policy to stop poachers, and the regrettable and violent deaths of the valiant anti-poaching teams who sacrifice their lives for the animals they love and guard. The impact of hunting, poaching, illegal animal trafficking (with the precious pangolin being a prime prize), carriage and import of animal parts and furs and skins, use of animal parts for medicinal purposes (including tiger and lion bones, rhino horns, and bear bile drained from living bears), habitat loss to support livestock and agriculture, blocking of natural corridors used for migration of animals and prey, lack of unified action about global warming which adversely affects animal habitats, lack of clarity and consistency of jurisdiction for animal protection and welfare, and lack of consistency with the justice systems and legislation to deter and punish perpetrators mean that the future for animals seems bleak.

Some countries in Africa have now banned hunting and poaching, recognising the value of their living wildlife as a natural resource, and hopefully this will help stem the epidemic of animal annihilation. America is reversing previously introduced laws banning imports of animal parts, and is reversing laws protecting bear and wolf mothers and their babies so that they can now legally be killed while they are hibernating, or with barbaric snares and traps and aerial shooting. Removing apex predators affects the whole ecosystem. Wolves were removed from Yellowstone National Park and the ecosystem is gradually recovering now that they have been reintroduced. There are countries where animals can be hunted or culled where there is no scientific evidence of plague or nuisance numbers, there is no conflict with livestock or humans, and no negative impact on the ecosystem. There is a huge money-making industry with selling hunting permits and licences, weapons and ammunition, hunting dogs, and other outfitting needs. While the laws condone killing, animal numbers will continue to plummet. If we hunt them all to extinction, we will be accountable for their loss and the subsequent emptiness.

Elephant numbers have decreased dramatically, but with recent international pressure banning the ivory trade and domestic markets, there is some hope. When I spoke to a representative "spokeselephant" for their commentary, I was told:

"We are killed every day for the ivory trade, which has supposedly closed down. We can't sustain this rate of loss to satisfy the bloodlust of hunters. The emotional trauma of the death of any member of our herd is immense for babies and adults. We feel these losses deeply. End the violence so we can roam in peace."

The cheetah population is at an all-time low, with numbers estimated at just over 7000 left in the wild. The cheetah who spoke to me on behalf of their species said:

"We have a tough life. Survival is a constant challenge. We don't mean to cause conflict. We need to provide food for our young. Help us maintain areas for our prey. We are fast, but we are fast disappearing."

Bears and cougars are being killed in considerable numbers in America. As well as being hunted by humans, they also have to contend with the humans' hunting dogs, who attack them. The bears and cougars are outnumbered and defenceless. The North Carolina Wildlife Resources Commission recently invited comment on their plans to increase the number of bear hunting permits by 4000 for the season. I very politely expressed my concerns about this, having spoken to a representative bear for their side of the story. I would have loved to have attended the decision-making process as a spokesperson for the bears.

The mother bear said:

"It is a struggle for our cubs to survive to adolescence and independence. If we get killed, our cubs starve to death without us there to provide for them. The hunting dogs cause us intense pain when they attack – we instinctively fight back to defend our cubs and some of the dogs get injured. We are now living in constant stress hounded by the dogs and their keepers."

The situation for lions is complex. The lion numbers have also diminished significantly. There is a whole industry now of "canned hunting" established purposely to meet the demand of trophy hunters. From my understanding, the hunting organisations breed their own lions, and they claim that they are not impacting on wild lion numbers, however wild lions continue to be hunted and killed. With the "canned hunting" industry, lion cubs are separated from their mothers and sent elsewhere where they can be looked after and generate profit for the temporary carers through petting and lion walks for tourists who are naïve about what is actually happening. I have spoken with people who raved about the experience of walking with the lions, and genuinely thought they were helping with their rehabilitation. Once they are older, the lions are returned to the hunting lodges where they are killed by trophy hunters. Their heads and skins are taken as trophies, and the lion meat and lion bones are sold for profit. There has been an increased demand for lion bones for medicinal purposes as the tiger bone supply has dwindled with the reduction of the tiger population. Ignoring the ethical implications of breeding animals to be killed for sport and duping the unsuspecting tourists, there are huge implications for the lions.

The lions say:

"We are exploited for money making. We don't have a quality life. There is no freedom. We are not truly wild. Our mothers mourn the loss of the cubs when they are removed too young, and never get to raise them to independence. Our cubs are wrenched from security and a nurturing family. They are frightened, and have no-one to comfort them. This is not living. This is existing. We are not respected and we are not valued as living beings – we die to generate money for humans. Our tolerance for this situation is not high. Is yours?"

Despite the global response to the death of popular lion Cecil who was deliberately lured from the protection of his reserve for trophy hunting, disturbingly there are ongoing reports of lions being killed after being lured from the safety of their 'protected' reserves. Poaching of other animals is also occurring in reserves. Sadly being in a reserve does not mean that animals are truly protected despite the best efforts of anti-poaching teams and guards.

The race to save the rhino is not over, but there are still many hurdles. They are still being killed and poached in unprecedented numbers for their horns, which are ground into powder for traditional Chinese medicines, alleged anti-hangover cures, and as a status symbol. Let me emphasise that point – a rhino death occurs to help a human recover from excessive drinking. In some parks and reserves now, the staff are taking unorthodox steps to prevent the rhino killings by either pre-emptively removing the horns, or using a fluorescent dye to paint the horns, which doesn't harm the rhino but makes the horns valueless for the market.

My "spokesrhino" shared the rhino contingent's views:

"Having our horns removed to keep us safe or painting them affects our beauty and we lose our identity – we are known for our horns. When we are killed for our horns, the adults after passing over grieve for the missed opportunity to raise their young, and are distressed by seeing them alone and unprotected. They didn't choose to die an unnatural death and didn't choose to abandon their children. The orphans mourn the loss of their parent. The fortunate few who are rescued have some quality of life, but the remainder who are immature in their progress to independence and are defenceless face certain death as they cannot survive on their own."

I had tears welling receiving this message. I could feel their overwhelming grief with the tragic reality they endure because of us. We may not all be hunters and poachers and rhino horn end users, but while there is a demand for rhino horn and our laws allow it, we are collectively responsible for forcing change.

I had the privilege of communicating with Sudan, the last remaining male northern white rhino, before he passed away in March this year (2018). He was 45, which is elderly for a rhino, his health had been declining, and people around the world were sending well wishes and energetic healing.

Sudan said at the time that he "feels really special and thanks everyone for their prayers" and he is "aware of the love and healing energy being sent".

He rallied for a few days after that, was more mobile and went outdoors in his boma.

He was happy to speak with me soon after he passed over.

He said he didn't want to leave the people looking after him, but said it was time for him to go. He now feels eternally young with no restrictions.

He is so humble and said he was very touched that his life and death have affected so many people.

When I asked him if he had a specific message, he said: "It's not too late, there is time to make a difference, we can change things for the better. Lead the charge!" He then showed me an image of him charging across a vast expanse of grassy land and it was wonderful to see him moving so comfortably and at speed. He truly is a beautiful soul.

When I asked if he had any additional messages for this book, he said: "Harmony and peace. Humans can orchestrate it: they have the knowledge, the science, and the motivation. A united force can achieve miracles."

Although the animals have painted an honest, heartfelt, compelling, and dire picture of today's situation, it doesn't have to stay that way. Through combining efforts across multiple agencies we can achieve legislation changes, we can quarantine land and corridors to maintain habitats, we can educate communities so that they can co-exist in harmony with animals and have sustainable incomes, we can advance our agriculture methods to be efficient with less land, we can educate our children to respect animals, we can translate the findings of science and research into practical animal conservation, and we can make a difference for animals. We need cohesion, collaboration, and motivation, knowing that the animals will be applauding our efforts.

We have the power to make extinction extinct.

CHAPTER 9

Return to Eden

How can you make a difference for the animals?

- Tell the animals that you live with that you love them. You may feel weird doing this at first but they will understand exactly what you are saying and will appreciate it, and it will strengthen their relationship with you. I tell my cats frequently that I love them and that I am grateful that they are in my life and have chosen to come back and support and teach me. We shouldn't take them for granted. They are in our life for a reason and whether they are with us for a short time or in for the long haul, every day that they are here is a gift.

- Enrol in an animal communication course. There are numerous teachers around the world offering face-to-face workshops or online courses. I have done both – different teachers have different experiences and approaches, but the keys are being open to receiving messages, trusting and not doubting what you hear, and practising! I chat to my cats regularly, but also spend as much time as I can in zoos talking to the animals, and chatting to other people's animals.

- Support animal conservation or animal rescue organisations or animal refuges. There are many organisations doing much needed research, working with local communities and lobbying governments to better protect animals and their habitats, rescuing orphans and other animals from inappropriate care, and educating our future generations on the value of animals and how we can ensure survival and co-habitation. I am aware that there are many organisations that do this valuable work and receive no government funding. They rely on donations and sponsorships and fundraising to keep on keeping on. Your financial support will inspire them.

  Please refer to the Resource section for organisations that I follow on Facebook and support.

  I recently attended a talk given by a former zoo cheetah keeper who is now working with Cheetah Conservation Botswana. They too rely on donations but are achieving great outcomes for the diminishing cheetah population. They are working with farmers and supplying trained dogs to protect their livestock. This means that the cheetahs don't attack the livestock animals, and the farmers don't have their livelihood threatened, and therefore don't need to kill the cheetahs. A lot of work is done with education in the community to raise awareness of the plight of cheetahs, and looking at ways communities can benefit from sharing their habitat, including ecotourism. Education in schools and communities is paramount in promoting why we should protect animals and generate sustainable incomes from their existence. This multi-faceted approach could be applied to animal conservation efforts around the world.

- You can "sponsor" or "adopt" an animal knowing that your dollars are contributing to the preservation and protection of species for the future. Many organisations offer animal-related merchandise to generate funds, including community handmade objects as a replacement economy for the former hunting of animals and repurposing of their habitats for other uses, including agriculture. I now buy animal sponsorships as Christmas presents for my family; gifts that I know are making a practical difference to animals around the world.

- Visit ethical zoos and introduce children to the wonders of Mother Nature. Many of the private zoos rely on visitor admission fees and purchases to fund animal food, medications, animal accommodation, and staff salaries to care for the animals. You can buy annual passes which means that the zoos have predictable income to plan with, and you get value for money with multiple visits.

- Lobby politicians and governments to tighten laws on importing animal body parts (including skins and furs), unethical culling, hunting, and poaching.

- Lobby governments to take action to reverse global warming as it is impacting significantly on animal habitats.

- Lobby governments to raise penalties for animal abuse.

- Sign petitions. There are many petition organisations on platforms such as Facebook seeking online support for animal welfare causes, including liberating mistreated animals from circuses, closing zoos where animals are not well looked after, stopping the use of animals for medicines, e.g. bear bile, banning import and markets for animal parts (including rhino horns and ivory), saying no to wearing animal furs and skins, and saying no to palm oil products.

- Support eco-tourism. If you can, spend time with animals in the wild, and contribute to local communities who are making concerted efforts to co-exist with animals.

- Hope and pray for a new world, where we co-exist in harmony with animals, sharing Earth's resources and lands.

Afterword

Words cannot express the utter devastation I feel seeing the impact humanity has had on our wild animals. They are noble, they transcend judgement, and they are silently moving closer to extinction.

Their words when I interviewed them for this book moved me. Their reliance on us to help them is undeniable. They need us to speak up and advocate for them.

I trust that you too are moved by their stories and inspired to take action.

For our animals in zoos there is hope for survival of species with coordinated global animal husbandry and responsible breeding plans where zoos can sustain new life. The mind shift to operating conscious zoos can only see conditions improve for animals so that they can achieve a better quality of life.

For those of you who are animals' humans, I trust that having a deeper understanding about why your animal is here, why they are with you, and knowing that you can communicate with them on a telepathic level will totally change your relationship with them, and that your experience will be the richer for it.

Animals are my passion. It is my purpose to raise awareness about animals and evolve understanding of animal consciousness so that we can value and respect them, co-exist in harmony with them, and grow from their wisdom and love.

Thank you for finding the bridge to Animal Consciousness.

Annie Bourke

The Cosmic Heart Intuitive

Acknowledgements

Thank you to my wonderful cats who fill each day with joy. I'm blessed to have you in my life, inspiring and guiding me. Thank you for your love, humour, wisdom, protection, and patience. I love you.

Thank you to all of the animals who contributed to this book. Your words moved me, and I trust that your words of wisdom and insights will inspire more people to take action on your behalf. Writing this book has been part of my life purpose – the essence of what I am here for expressed in words to create this book and through it to make a real difference for all animals. It is an honour and a huge responsibility to speak for you.

Thank you to Tracey, Renee, Pete, Maddy, Teagan, Amy, and Kym for your dedicated and excellent veterinary care of my fur family.

Thank you to the talented Ken, Beck, and John at Zoo Studios for so expertly and exquisitely capturing the magnificence of my fur family in your stunning photography.

A huge thank you to Dave Thompson, 'Inspirational Book Writers' mastermind and founder, for your wisdom, guidance, support, humour, and patience helping my book become a reality and helping me achieve my dream through contributing to a better world for animals.

Thank you also to the inspirational 'Inspirational Book Writers Retreat' crew – Davina, AJ and Heather – you did an outstanding job providing support, nourishment for body and soul, and wise counsel.

Thank you to my publishing team for their behind the scenes craftsmanship with editing, formatting and design. I appreciate your teamwork in turning my raw manuscript into the completed book.

Resources

Animal messages, animal totems, understanding animal wisdom and healing

Scott Alexander King   http://animaldreaming.com/

Animal photography

Zoo Studios   https://www.zoostudio.com.au/
                 https://www.facebook.com/ZooStudioPhotography

Essential oils

Dr Melissa Shelton   http://oilyvet.com/
                        http://www.animaleo.info/oilyvet/
                        (Desk reference for oils and animals)

Funeral urns

Furry Souls   https://www.petcremationurns.com.au/
                 https://www.facebook.com/FurrySoulsCremationUrns/

Organisations involved with animal issues and conservation

African Wildlife Foundation   https://www.awf.org/

Cheetah Conservation Botswana	http://www.cheetahconservationbotswana.org/
Cheetah Conservation Fund	https://www.facebook.com/CCFcheetah/
Cheetah Conservation Fund Australia	www.cheetah.org.au
Global Sanctuary for Elephants	https://globalelephants.org/
Justice for Cecil the Lion	https://www.justiceforcecilthelionofficial.com/
Ol Pejeta Conservancy	http://www.olpejetaconservancy.org/
Polar Bears International	https://polarbearsinternational.org/
Snow Leopard Trust	https://www.snowleopard.org

Contact Annie

My business, The Cosmic Heart Intuitive, is based north of Brisbane in Queensland, Australia.

Please contact me for further information about my services:

- Conversations with animals (present or passed over). For national and international clients, these can be arranged using Skype or by email with photo readings. Please note that conversations are subject to the animal agreeing to converse - it is their choice.
- Animal consultations (e.g. behavioural or health issues with animals in zoos)
- Vibrational energy healing support sessions for humans and animals (intuitive healing including Reiki, crystal therapy, aromatherapy, mediumship and clairvoyance).
- Event presentations
- Workshops

For enquiries and bookings, please email me at CHIntuitive@bigpond.com

You can also follow me on Facebook:
https://www.facebook.com/TheCosmicHeartIntuitive/

Notes

Notes

Notes

Notes

Notes

Notes

Notes

Notes

Notes

Notes

Notes